I0087390

The Not-So-Impossible
Book of Revelation

It begins with a voice from heaven.

Kathy Nosal

Misula Press

Orlando, FL

© 2018 Kathy Nosal

All rights reserved. This book or any portion thereof may not be reproduced or used in any manner whatsoever without the express written permission of the publisher except for the use of brief quotations in a book review.

Disclaimer: The Publisher and the Author make no representations or warranties with respect to the accuracy or completeness of the contents of this work and specifically disclaim all warranties, including without limitation warranties of fitness for a particular purpose. No warranty may be created or extended by sales or promotional materials. The advice and strategies contained herein may not be suitable for every situation. This work is sold with the understanding that the Publisher is not engaged in rendering legal, accounting, or other professional services. If professional assistance is required, the services of a competent professional person should be sought. Neither the Publisher nor the Author shall be liable for damages arising here from. The fact that an organization or website is referred to in this work as a citation and/or a potential source of further information does not mean that the Author or the Publisher endorses the information the organization or website may provide or recommendations it may make. Further, readers should be aware that Internet websites listed in this work may have changed or disappeared between when this work was written and when it is read. For permission requests, contact the publisher.

"Scripture taken from the NEW AMERICAN STANDARD BIBLE®, Copyright © 1960,1962,1963,1968,1971,1972,1973,1975,1977,1995 by The Lockman Foundation. Used by permission."

Scripture quotations marked (NIV) are taken from the Holy Bible, New International Version®, NIV®. Copyright © 1973, 1978, 1984, 2011 by Biblica, Inc.™ Used by permission of Zondervan. All rights reserved worldwide. www.zondervan.com The "NIV" and "New International Version" are trademarks registered in the United States Patent and Trademark Office by Biblica, Inc.™

Unless otherwise indicated, all Scripture quotations are taken from THE MESSAGE, copyright © 1993, 1994, 1995, 1996, 2000, 2001, 2002 by Eugene H. Peterson. Used by permission of NavPress. All rights reserved. Represented by Tyndale House Publishers, Inc.

Scripture quotations marked (NLT) are taken from the Holy Bible, New Living Translation, copyright ©1996, 2004, 2015 by Tyndale House Foundation. Used by permission of Tyndale House Publishers, Inc., Carol Stream, Illinois 60188. All rights reserved.

Printed in the United States of America
Cover photo: Kathy Nosal

First edition published 2018
10 9 8 7 6 5 4 3 2 1
Nosal, Kathy
The Not-So-Impossible Book of Revelation / Kathy Nosal

ISBN-13: 978-0-578-43683-8

Misula Press

To Mark

Love you forever.

For everything that was written in the past was written to teach us,

so that, through the endurance taught in the Scriptures and

the encouragement they provide we might have hope.

Romans 15:4 (NIV)

Table of Contents

The Second Study

Blessed is the one who reads aloud the words of this prophecy, and blessed are those who hear it and take to heart what is written in it, because the time is near.

Revelation 1:3 (NIV)

Questions

What is the book of Revelation about? Write whatever comes to mind, anything at all.

What questions do you have about the book of Revelation? Write them below.

The Not-So-Impossible Book of Revelation

Revelation illustrates the eternal battle of good versus evil. In an earthly sense, the book of Revelation may seem a bit crazy. In a spiritual sense, it is not.

Is it a complicated book? Yes, it is hard to understand in places, but at its core it is simple. It shows two choices and two destinations. God or no God. Heaven or hell.

When it comes to studying Revelation, you won't know it all, no one does. The apostle John, the writer of Revelation, is given a command to *"Write on a scroll what you see and send it to the seven churches"* (New International Version, Rev. 1:11). The command is not to understand what he sees, but to write what he sees.

Let's remember this, but with a tweak – *read* the book and see what you see. Sure, you may not understand the meaning of all that you read, but you can know what you read.

What do I mean by you can know what you read? Let's say you come across an article about the book of Revelation. It mentions the four letters to the four churches. You will soon learn that is incorrect. There are seven letters to seven churches in Revelation. Even if you do not understand what is in the letters, you know there are seven, not four. You know enough to distinguish truth from an error. Yes, you can know what you read.

Too many people talk themselves out of reading the book of Revelation because they falsely believe they aren't smart enough. Or know enough. Not true! Don't be intimidated by what you think others can do but you cannot. There is no diploma, degree, or education requirement to read and study Revelation. Or, the bible for that matter.

This is not a slight at priests, pastors or others who have a formal biblical education. Is it good to listen and read from bible teachers and pastors? Yes! Is it okay to read books or websites on the subject? Yes! I have and continue to learn from others who are biblically based teachers and writers. And, I am grateful to all of them as they have helped me learn and grow.

Yet, we need to learn for ourselves and not let others tell us what to believe. Why? Discernment. So you can discern biblical truth from error. God will lead us in the correct ways. It may be through other people, reading a book, or listening to a sermon. We just have to be alert, and reading the bible keeps us alert to God.

This study guide is for you to learn and discover on your own. This guide is just that, a guide. It is not about what I say as the guide's author, but for you to discover on your own what you see God saying.

Reading and learning what is in the bible is about God. It is for all of us to know, so whatever your background, the bible and what it says is for you! You can study it, on your own, for yourself and learn.

As you study Revelation, keep this question in mind – How big do you view God? A big God has no box. Often, we have a box of understanding and try to fit God into our box. Instead, approach Revelation, or any bible study, as a way to enlarge your box to include the bigness of God.

Three Questions

Revelation brings about many questions; here are three that come up often.

Question #1 – Is Revelation Literal or Symbolic Writing?

Does Revelation mean what it literally says or is it symbolic?

Yes to both.

First, read Revelation literally. Be mindful of what you see in the text. You may be surprised that when you slow down and read, you can understand more than you realize now. When you come to a difficult passage, ask yourself, "What does the verse literally say?"

Then, further explore a passage by asking,

· Is this confusing because the context and words are hard to understand?
· Is this confusing because the words together just don't make sense to me?
· Is this difficult because it illustrates something? (a symbol)
· Is the illustration confusing?

See if you can fine tune what aspect is confusing. But, don't try to make an answer when you do not have one. Don't get frustrated. It is possible as you continue to read, you will see something that helps you understand. Even if that does not happen, staying stuck is not a good option, so just move on. You can always go back and revisit a challenging passage.

Question #2 – Is Revelation a Chronological Account?

There are many beliefs on this and volumes written around these various viewpoints. In general, the views are,

A. Yes, it is in chronological order

B. No, it describes something at different times and is not in order

C. Both A and B.

What is not disputable is that there are time indicators. When you see words and phrases like,

- Then
- After this
- After these things
- Immediately

These are time indicators within passages. These are important, look for them and note their context.

Question #3 – Is Revelation Past, Present, or Future?

There are a few prevailing views on this question. But, I am not going to go into them here because I do not want you to start with a preconceived notion if you don't already have one. If you do have a belief about this that is fine, but I do ask you keep an open mind during this bible study. Your views may change based on what you discover here. (Mine did after doing an in-depth study)

My suggestion is that after you complete this study, ideally, after you finish both *The First Study* and *The Second Study*, write what your view is – past, present or future. Then, consult bible commentaries with varying opinions to see what they say. This way you are reading another's observations based on your thinking, not letting someone else's opinion guide your thinking first.

How to Use This Guide

What to Expect

In *The Not-So-Impossible Book of Revelation,* you will,

- Increase your awareness of Revelation's message
- Know things in Revelation you thought impossible to know
- Be comfortable not understanding it all (because no one does)

There is no answer key in this guide. You do not need one. Don't let that scare you; this is not about getting answers from someone else. It is finding them for yourself. The answers are found in doing the guide activities, kind of like an open book test, but this is not a test! There are also reflective questions that give you a chance to think about what you are reading.

How This Guidebook Works

This one book has two study guides designed to do in order. There is,

1. *The First Study*

The goal of *The First Study* is to lead you through the book of Revelation. This first study will help you know and be aware of Revelation's message. You will go through the book of Revelation to see what it says. It is an overview.

2. *The Second Study*

It is likely that after going through *The First Study,* you will want to delve deeper into the book of Revelation. That is the reason for *The Second Study.* It builds on your learning and insights with more in-depth activities. The good news is that you do not need to get another study guide. And, all your work from *The First Study* is here, all in one place.

You can also do the studies at the same time by doing both chapter ones, chapter twos and so on. Do this if you want to do a single in-depth study.

How You Will Learn

You will use critical thinking and discovery learning. Discovery learning is high-value learning because it is personal. When you were a child, did your mother tell you not to touch the hot stove? And you listened to her until one day you couldn't contain yourself and you felt the hot stove. Ouch! You discovered the hot stove! Discovery learning makes an impression, and you are less likely to forget it. The bible is perfect for discovery learning.

What You Need

A Bible

This guide uses the *New International Version (NIV)* translation, so that is what I recommend first. If you use another version that is fine, the important thing is to have a bible to do this study.

A Note About Bible Translations

Bible translations fall along a spectrum. At one end of the spectrum are word-for-word translations. These are closest to the original Hebrew, Aramaic and Greek texts. At the other end of the spectrum are paraphrase translations that express the idea in the writing.

Range of Bible Translations

TYPE of TRANSLATION:
Word for word →   Thought for thought →   Paraphrase
BIBLE TRANSLATION
NASB............NKJV...................NIV...............NLT...............The MSG

Bible Translation Key:

- · NASB – New American Standard Bible
- · NKJV – New King James Version
- · NIV – New International Version
- · NLT – New Living Translation
- · The MSG – The Message

Let's look at a verse to see the difference in translations.

	New American Standard Bible (NASB)	New International Version (NIV)	The Message (MSG)
Translation Type	Word for Word (closest to original text)	Thought for Thought	A Paraphrase (expresses the idea of the text)
Revelation 1:3	Blessed is he who reads and those who hear the words of the prophecy, and heed the things which are written in it; for the time is near.	Blessed is the one who reads aloud the words of this prophecy, and blessed are those who hear it and take to heart what is written in it, because the time is near.	How blessed the reader! How blessed the hearers and keepers of these oracle words, all the words written in this book! Time is just about up.

1. What differences stand out in these translations?

2. Compare the word-for-word NASB translation with The Message (MSG) paraphrase translation. How do the two translations differ? How are they the same?

So what is the best bible translation? The best translation is the one that gets you to read the bible!

Pens, Highlighters, Pencils

Color pens, color pencils, color markers to mark and write in your bible. For the color pens and markers make sure they are ones that do not bleed through paper. Gel highlighters and pens work well for this.

What You Will Do – *The First Study*

Each chapter has three main activities:

- *Read* – The chapter's reading assignment.

- *Think* – A question or statement related to the reading. It is to get you thinking about some aspect of what you just read.

- *Do* – Questions and activities related to the reading. You will discover the answers in the assigned text. As mentioned, kind of like an open book test, except this is not a test!

Making Marks in Your Bible

Don't get overwhelmed by this. Underline, circle, draw a box around – mark in a way that is meaningful for you. Marking text helps you see patterns in the text.

Answer Questions

You will answer questions based on what you read in the bible. You uncover biblical truths by doing this.

Draw What You Read/See

Drawing what you read and see in your mind helps to understand the words. I find this activity helpful even though I cannot draw. Have fun with this!

What You Will Do – *The Second Study*

You will need the same tools, but the activities are different. Here is a glance at what you will do; details are in *The Second Study* introduction.

Word Studies

A word study looks at the definition of a word in its original meaning. Word studies provide context.

Cross-Referencing Verses

Cross-referencing looks at what the bible says about a topic, event or person in more than one place in the bible. Cross-referencing expands your understanding.

Activities

Activities include completing charts, timelines, answering questions and reflective thinking.

You Can Do This!

Read without fear. Don't stop if you get stuck, instead skip that part and keep moving. I cannot stress this enough. Do not give up, continue on. Tell yourself, "I will come back to this later." As you study, you will understand more of Revelation than you think.

Yes, you can do this!

The
First
Study

Keep an open mind.

Don't be afraid to see what you see.

You will have questions.

Everyone does.

You won't know it all.

No one does.

These are God's words, for us.

He wants us to read them.

All of us, including you.

Go for it.

Chapter 1: It Begins

Revelation 1:1-20

This is no wordy beginning. Revelation begins with the power of brevity. This book's unveiling is from God to Jesus. Why? So Jesus could show his followers the things which must soon take place. *Must* soon take place. *Must* – it has to happen.

This book comes with a blessing to anyone who reads it, who hears it and takes to heart what it says. That is an important thing to note, *the takes to heart part.* God wants you to know what it means so you can then take it to heart. It is not to remain a mystery.

READ

In your bible, read Revelation 1:1-20.

THINK

Who and what is the revelation about?

DO

Looking in Revelation 1, complete the following questions and activities.

1. Underline, circle or mark in some way, the following in Revelation 1.
   · Jesus
   · God
   · John
   · Spirit

2. Review your markings of Jesus in Revelation 1. What do you learn about Jesus?

3. Review your markings of God in Revelation 1. What do you learn about God?

4. Who is John?

5. Where is John? Why is he there?

6. What is John doing? What is his state or condition?

7. What are the two things John is commanded to do?

8. What did John see, hear, look at?

9. Review your marking of Spirit in Revelation 1. What did you learn?

10. Where are the seven cities of the seven churches?

11. Describe the "someone like a son of man."

12. How does the "like a son of man" describe himself?

Fill-in-the-Blank

13. The 7 golden lampstands are _____.

14. The 7 stars are _____.

15. The 7 spirits are _____. (location)

16. Who is coming in the clouds?

17. Who will mourn on the earth? Why?

MY NOTES

Write any notes, insights or questions you have here so you can ponder or revisit at another time.

NOTE OF INTEREST: WHAT THE BIBLE TELLS US ABOUT JOHN

He was a brother to James (Matthew 4:21)

His father was Zebedee (Matthew 4:21)

He was an apostle of Jesus. (Matthew 10:2; Mark 3:17)

He was part of Jesus' three-person inner circle. (Mark 5:37; Mark 9:2)

He was uneducated, untrained but confident in Jesus. (Acts 4:13)

He was a brother and fellow partaker in the tribulation. (Revelation 1:9)

At the time of Revelation, he was on the island of Patmos. (Revelation 1:9)

(What the Bible Tells us About John is an example of cross-referencing.)

Chapter 2: The Letters to the Churches, part 1

Revelation 2:1-29

We now know about the lampstands and what they represent. Can you see that God wants us to know things?

Revelation chapters 2 and 3 are individual letters to seven churches in Asia. Each letter is personal. Each one contains information for that church. Some churches receive praise, some a scolding. All are given a message to its overcomers.

Notice that each letter gives a different description of Jesus. They are not competing descriptions: they are complements. Jesus is not one dimensional, He can communicate with anyone willing to listen and accept Him.

READ

In your bible, read Revelation 2:1-29.

THINK

What are your thoughts about attending a church? What does "going to church" mean to you?

DO

Looking in Revelation 2, complete the following questions and activities.

The Letter to the Church of Ephesus (Revelation 2:1-6)

1. Describe the one who is talking.

2. Is there praise? If yes, what is it?

3. Is there a reprimand? If yes, what is it?

4. Is there a command or consequence? If yes, what?

5. What is the promise?

6. What is the Ephesians first love?

NOTE OF INTEREST: THE CITY OF EPHESUS

Ephesus, an ancient coastal city where the main inland route started and ended. It was home to large temples to gods. One of them, the temple of Artemis, was one of the seven wonders of the ancient world and was a source of a lot of income. There was a sheltered harbor and over time the harbor silted up. By the 9th century Ephesus was an inland city, and eventually it was abandoned.

The Letter to the Church of Smyrna (Revelation 2:7-13)

7. Describe the one who is talking.

8. Is there praise? If yes, what is it?

9. Is there a reprimand? If yes, what is it?

10. Is there a command or consequence? If yes, what?

11. What is the promise?

12. Who will put some of them in prison?

NOTE OF INTEREST: THE CITY OF SMYRNA

A wealthy city, Smyrna had a deep sheltered harbor. Along with Ephesus, it was an important coastal city. It had a deep bond with Rome before Christ and worshipped Rome as a spiritual power. Smyrna was loyal to the Romans and known for its Jews hatred for Christians. Jews were exempt from worshiping the Roman emperor and this left Christians open to persecution. Smyrna was famous for science, medicine, and grand buildings. Today, the city of Izmir, Turkey is on this site.

The Letter to the Church of Pergamum (Revelation 2:12-17)

13. Describe the one who is talking.

14. Is there praise? If yes, what is it?

15. Is there a reprimand? If yes, what is it?

16. Is there a command or consequence? If yes, what?

17. What is the promise?

18. Who lives and has his throne in Pergamum?

NOTE OF INTEREST: THE CITY OF PERGAMUM

One of the largest cities in the region, it was wealthy, beautiful and with lots of temples. Here also the Roman imperial cult was established and held importance in paganism. It had the sanctuary of Asclepius, the healer-god which drew people from other parts of the world. In Smyrna, politics and paganism were intertwined and unifying factors.

The Letter to the Church of Thyatira (Revelation 2:18-29)

19. Describe the one who is talking.

20. Is there praise? If yes, what is it?

21. Is there a reprimand? If yes, what is it?

22. Is there a command or consequence? If yes, what?

23. What is the promise?

24. What is Jezebel given time to do? What do she and her followers do?

NOTE OF INTEREST: THE CITY OF THYATIRA

Known for its pagan trade guilds and bronze smiths, it had more trade guilds than any other Asian city. Trade guild meals were dedicated to pagan deities as well as emperor worship. Not having a guild membership could mean a loss of income. The necessity of membership in a trade guild invited Christians to compromise and opened the door to many temptations. Thyatira is modern day Akhisar, Turkey.

MY NOTES

Write any notes, insights or questions you have here so you can ponder or revisit at another time.

Chapter 3: The Letters to the Churches, part 2

Revelation 3:1-22

Here are the last three letters to the seven churches of Asia. Can you see how Jesus speaks personally to each church? These are not form letters; these are personal. He knows each church and talks to them in ways they understand.

Think of people you know and their different personalities. Think about how you interact with:

- a shy person
- a non-stop talker
- a liar
- someone like you
- someone the opposite of you

While we may struggle with how to interact with different people, Jesus does not. He can and does relate to each of us where we are.

READ

In your bible, read Revelation 3:1-22.

THINK

What do you say to "the church" in general, or to a specific church, about the following?

Praise for the church:

Reprimand for the church:

DO

Looking in Revelation 3, complete the following questions and activities.

The Letter to the Church of Sardis (Revelation 3:1-6)

1. Describe the one who is talking.

2. Is there praise? If yes, what is it?

3. Is there a reprimand? If yes, what is it?

4. Is there a command or consequence? If yes, what?

5. What is the promise?

6. There is a book mentioned, what is the name of it?

NOTE OF INTEREST: THE CITY OF SARDIS

Sardis became the center of the Persian administration in the west. It was the capital of Lydia with wealth, fame and paganism. During the Roman Empire, it was one of the most prosperous cities of the region. There is no mention of persecution and it seems the Jewish and Christian communities coexisted.

The Letter to the Church of Philadelphia (Revelation 3:7-13)

7. Describe the one who is talking.

8. Is there praise? If yes, what is it?

9. Is there a reprimand? If yes, what is it?

10. Is there a command or consequence? If yes, what?

11. What is the promise?

12. Who are the liars? What synagogue do they belong to?

NOTE OF INTEREST: THE CITY OF PHILADELPHIA

Philadelphia had no natural defenses. It became a Roman territory and then part of the Byzantine Empire. It was and is famous for its wine. The god of wine, Dionysus (Greek), and Bacchus (Roman) were worshipped here. Philadelphia's nickname was Little Athens.

The Letter to the Church of Laodicea (Revelation 3:14-22)

13. Describe the one who is talking.

14. Is there praise? If yes, what is it?

15. Is there a reprimand? If yes, what is it?

16. Is there a command or consequence? If yes, what?

17. What is the promise?

18. What does it mean to be lukewarm?

NOTE OF INTEREST: THE CITY OF LAODICEA

Laodicea was near the river Lycus, a tributary of the river Meander. This water was a significant source of the region's agricultural wealth. It was an important trade and military route and became part of the Roman Empire. It also was in an earthquake-prone area, so natural disasters were not uncommon. It was as a medical center where doctors specialized in ear and eye diseases. Wool was also a much-traded product.

You and the Letters to the Churches

19. What church letter do you identify with the most? Is there one that has your name on it?

20. Why?

Pause Button #1

Good work! You studied Revelation's first three chapters! Let's stop for a moment so you can gather your thoughts before moving on. So, do you have questions? Great - questions are good. It shows you are engaged. Keep at it.

1. What do you know from studying Revelation 1-3? Not necessarily understand, but what do you know or are aware of?

2. Did you gain an insight or a new perspective on something? If yes, what?

3. What did you learn?

Chapter 4: Heaven's Throne Room

Revelation 4:1-5:14

Here is a dramatic scene change. Think big, outside of conventional parameters to imagine what John sees and writes. John uses,

Imagery

·   "like an emerald rainbow"
·   "something like a sea of glass"

Specifics

·   24 elders
·   four living creatures

As you read, notice phrases:

·   Like a…
·   I (John) heard, I saw, I looked

Read big, think big. The next time you are looking up at the sky, think about what you read here.

READ

In your bible, read Revelation 4:1-5:14.

THINK

What does heaven look like to you?

DO

Looking in Revelation 4:1-5:14, complete the following questions and activities.

1. In Revelation 4, underline, circle or mark in some way these time phrases. Then, make a list of these phrases with what comes after it (*i.e., After these things I heard a voice ...*):

   ·   After these things/After this

   ·   What must take place after these things/What must take place after this

   ·   At once/Immediately

2. In Revelation 4, underline, circle or mark in some way the following:

·   The Spirit. What do you learn about the Spirit?

·   God/Lord God. What do you learn about God?

·   The Lamb. What do you learn about the Lamb?

3. Where is John?

4. Describe the One sitting on the throne.

5. Describe the throne, what is around it? Coming out of it?

6. Describe the 24 elders. What do they do?

7. Describe the four living creatures.

· The first living creature looks like…

· The second living creature looks like…

· The third living creature looks like…

· The fourth living creature looks like…

8. What characteristics do all four creatures have in common?

9. What do the golden bowls of incense contain?

10. How many angels are there? Where are they?

11. What do every creature in heaven and on earth sing?

12. Circle three words that, for you, best describe the throne room in heaven.

Unending	Colorful	Scary	Real
Make believe	Holy	Beautiful	Overwhelming
Weird	Alive	Untrue	Loud

13. Write a description of the throne room in heaven using these three words.

MY NOTES

Write any notes, insights or questions you have here so you can ponder or revisit at another time.

Chapter 5: The Seals

Revelation 6:1-17

The breaking of the seals reveals fantastic events. Yet, the unsealing is not chaotic; there is an order to things.

The first seal is broken,

then the second,

then the third...

With the breaking of each seal, there is an explanation. Just read what the words say. It's okay to read it over and over if you need to. Read like this...

· The first seal is broken, *and this happens.*
· The second seal is broken, *and this happens.*

And so on.

READ

In your bible, read Revelation 6:1-17.

THINK

Think of the events in Revelation 6 as a video. What are your feelings and thoughts as you watch the video? What is your reaction when each seal is broken and you see the results?

DO

Looking in Revelation 6:1-17, complete the following questions and activities.

1. Describe the four living creatures' role in unsealing the first four seals. What do they say? Who do they talk to?

2. Who are the souls underneath the altar? What is their request?

3. What has or had to happen for their request to be fulfilled?

4. List the events in Revelation 6:12-17.

5. List the people in Revelation 6:15-16.

6. What did the people in these verses do?

7. Who/What are they hiding from?

Note of Interest: Money, Food, and Wine

Denarius – A small Roman silver coin, its value varied at different times.

Wheat –Any edible grain, but usually wheat. Wheat was more expensive than barley.

Barley – The grain eaten by the common person and also used as food for horses. Notice the cost for three quarts of barley or one quart of wheat is a denarius.

Oil (olives) and Wine (grapes) – Olives and grapes are not annual crops and take years to recover if destroyed.

Did you notice the command not to damage the oil and the wine?

MY NOTES

Write any notes, insights or questions you have here so you can ponder or revisit at another time.

Chapter 6: The 144,000 and the Multitude

Revelation 7:1-17

Six of the seven seals are broken. We move to an interlude where we see two groups:

- 144,000 bondservants
- A multitude

There are a lot of things going on.

Slow down and read verse by verse.

Take your time.

READ

In your bible, read Revelation 7:1-17.

THINK

What do you know or have heard about the tribulation?

DO

Looking in Revelation 7:1-17, complete the following questions and activities.

1. Where are the 144,000 from?

2. Who makes up the multitude?

3. Where are those in white robes from?

4. Who is around the throne worshipping God?

5. List out the things that are "never again." (Rev 7:16)

6. List the things that the Lamb and God will do. (Rev 7:17)

7. Which is more appealing to you right now in your life? The *never again* list or the things that the Lamb and God will do? Why?

MY NOTES

Write any notes, insights or questions you have here so you can ponder or revisit at another time.

Chapter 7: The Trumpets

Revelation 8:1-9:21

The seventh seal is broken with some interesting results.

- Silence
- Seven trumpets
- Smoke of incense

Again, notice the orderliness – one trumpet sounds, then another and another.

Imagine the appearance of things in the world.

Reflect on how people respond.

What would your response be?

READ

In your bible, read Revelation 8:1-9:21.

THINK

What are your beliefs about prayer?

DO

Looking in Revelation 8:1-9:21, complete the following questions and activities.

1. What happens when the seventh seal is broken?

2. Where are the prayers of the saints?

3. List the things that are 1/3 affected.

4. What happens to people who do not have the seal of God on their foreheads?

5. What is the first woe?

6. Why were the four angels at the Euphrates released?

7. What are the three plagues out of the horses' mouths?

8. The rest of mankind worships demons and idols.

    ·   What are the idols made of?

    ·   Who creates idols?

    ·   What are the idols not able to do?

9. Based on Revelation 9:20-21, can an idol hear your prayers? Yes or No?

10. Read Habakkuk 2:18-20 and then answer the following.

    ·   What does the person who makes an idol trust in?
    ·   Can an idol speak? Yes or No
    ·   Can an idol breathe? Yes or No
    ·   Where is God?

11. Re-read Revelation 8:1-5. Can God hear your prayers?

Pause Button #2

Good work! Now you have studied nine chapters! Let's take another breather to gather your thoughts before moving on. Give thought to your answers here, it will help you realize what you have learned and bring to mind questions you have.

1. What do you know from studying Revelation 4-9? Not necessarily understand, but what do you know or are aware of?

2. What is your reaction to what you read in Revelation 4-9?

3. What did you learn?

Chapter 8: The Little Scroll

Revelation 10:1-11

Another interlude. Another scroll. Recall God held the previous scroll, and it was taken by Jesus the Lamb, in God's throne room.

This scroll is small and held by a strong angel. There are voices, noise from the heavens, and commands.

During this break from the trumpets sounding, John is given another command. Look for it.

READ

In your bible, read Revelation 10:1-11.

THINK

What do you believe about angels?

DO

Looking in Revelation 10:1-11, complete the following questions and activities.

1. Circle, underline or mark in some way "when" and "then". Then, write each *when* and *then* statement, in order of appearance.

2. List John's actions in Revelation 10.

3. Describe the mighty/strong angel.

4. What do the voices of the seven peals of thunder do?

5. What does the voice from heaven say?

6. **Fill-in-the-blank**

   The mighty angel says,

   "There will be_____.

7. What will happen when the seventh angel is about to sound?

8. John is told to do two things, what are they?

9. What, if anything, do these events in Revelation 10 say about humankind not knowing God's entire detailed plan? What do you think of this?

MY NOTES

Write any notes, insights or questions you have here so you can ponder or revisit at another time.

Chapter 9: The Two Witnesses

Revelation 11:1-19

We are no longer with the mighty angel. Now, John is given a task to do and then two witnesses appear. They are given powers. As you read look for, time designations (i.e., 1260 days).

At this point are you:

·   Amazed?

·   Overwhelmed?

·   Skeptical?

·   Convicted?

·   Convinced?

It's a lot to take in – but you can do it!

READ

In your bible, read Revelation 11:1-19.

THINK

What is a covenant? How is it different than a contract?

DO

Looking in Revelation 11:1-19, complete the following questions and activities.

1. What is given to John and what is he told to do?

2. List what you learn about the two witnesses.

3. What do the people on the earth do after the two witnesses die?

4. Who sees the two witnesses go up to heaven? How did they feel?

5. What is the second woe?

6. **Fill in the blanks**

(Rev 11:15) *The kingdom of the world has become*_____

_____*He will reign*_____

(Rev 11:18) *The time has for judging*_____

*and for rewarding*_____

7. What is in God's temple in heaven?

MY NOTES

Write any notes, insights or questions you have here so you can ponder or revisit at another time.

Chapter 10: War

Revelation 12:1-17

War, what is it good for? Absolutely nothing.

The above lyrics are from the song *War* recorded by Edwin Starr in 1970. It was a protest song against the Vietnam War.

Most of us agree with the sentiment that war is good for nothing. But, the war that takes place here is not a fight over land, money or riches. This war is a fight over souls and their final destination in eternity. It is a fight over wickedness and righteousness. Righteousness, that is being in right-standing with God.

There is imagery and symbolism, but there is also information that is plain and clear.

Just read and see what you see.

READ

In your bible, read Revelation 12:1-17.

THINK

Do you believe that Satan is real? Why or why not?

DO

Looking in Revelation12:1-17, complete the following questions and activities.

1. List what you see about each of these entities in Revelation 12:1-9; 13-17.

The woman	The great red dragon	The male child	Michael, the angel

2. Where did the war break out?

3. Who is fighting in the war?

4. Who lost their place in heaven? Where was he thrown down/hurled to?

5. How much time does the devil have?

6. Where is God?

7. Where is the devil?

8. Who does the dragon/devil pursue and make war against?

9. There are two side of this war. Michael is on one side of the war and the dragon on the other side. Describe each side's position – what are they fighting against? Who are they fighting for? (The answers are in Revelation 12.)

MY NOTES

Write any notes, insights or questions you have here so you can ponder or revisit at another time.

Chapter 11: The Dragon and the Beasts

Revelation 13:1-18

The dragon's saga continues. Now, two others join him and he gives them his authority.

What is going on?

Are lines being drawn?

READ

In your bible, read Revelation 13:1-18.

THINK

What does it mean to worship someone or something?

DO

Looking in Revelation 13:1-18, complete the following questions and activities.

1. *"Who can make war against him"* (Rev 13:4). What does this say to you about how people feel – emotionally and intellectually – about the first beast?

2. Where does the 2nd beast, the one out of the sea, get his authority?

3. What does the 2nd beast make people do?

4. What does a person need to have to calculate the number of the beast?

5. What is the number?

6. Who or what does the number represent?

7. Fill in the table.

	The Dragon	The First Beast	The Second Beast
Where is this entity?			
Where did this entity come from? (location)			
How does John describe this entity?			
Was authority given to this entity? Yes or no.			
What animal is in their description?			
Are they trustworthy? Why?			
Are they deceitful? Why?			

8. Summarize what you learned about the dragon, the first beast, and the second beast as a group. What is their common mission or goal?

Pause Button #3

You have completed 13 chapters and are more than halfway through Revelation! Time for another pause button.

1. What do you know from studying Revelation 10-13? Not necessarily understand, but what do you know or are aware of?

2. Did you gain an insight or a new perspective on something? If yes, what?

3. There is a lot of imagery – what is clear to you? What is confusing to you?

Chapter 12: Announcements

Revelation 14:1-20

In a way, this chapter is a promise to believers and non-believers. As you read, think about where you are —

- Am I with Jesus?
- Am I with the beast?
- I don't know.

There is a line here.

One line and two sides.

READ

In your bible, read Revelation 14:1-20.

THINK

What do you believe about saints?

DO

Looking in Revelation 14:1-20, complete the following questions and activities.

1. Who is standing on Mt Zion?

2. Where are the 144,000?

3. What do the 144,000 have on their foreheads?

4. What do those who dwell on the earth have on their foreheads?

5. There are three angels in Revelation 14:6-12 talking to those on earth. What do they say?

	Says…	Is this a warning? Yes or no.
1ˢᵗ angel		
2ⁿᵈ angel		
3ʳᵈ angel		

6. Complete the table.

	Who is their leader?	What are their characteristics?
The 144,000		
Those who dwell on earth		

7. Read Revelation 14:14-19. The first sickle cut harvests the earth as the earth is ripe. *Harvest* means to cut, reap. The second sickle cut gathers clusters of grapes. *Gather* means to collect, assemble. The grapes are then thrown into the winepress of God's wrath. What is the difference between the two sickle cuts? The difference between harvest and gather?

MY NOTES

Write any notes, insights or questions you have here so you can ponder or revisit at another time.

Chapter 13: Another Sign in Heaven

Revelation 15:1-8

Why is God angry?

One line. Two sides.

God is on one side of the line. Satan is on the other side.

Each one of us gets to choose our side.

READ

In your bible, read Revelation 15:1-8.

THINK

What is wrath?

DO

Looking in Revelation 15:1-8, complete the following questions and activities.

1. What is the great, marvelous sign?

2. How is God's wrath completed?

3. Why are those standing on a sea of glass victorious?

4. Describe God in Revelation 15:3-4.

5. What does John see in heaven?

6. What is in the seven golden bowls?

7. Where does the smoke come from?

8. Review your notes on the seven seals and the seven trumpets (Chapter 5 and Chapter 7 in this guide) and make notations on each one in the table below.

Number	Seal	Trumpet
1		
2		
3		
4		
5		
6		
7		

MY NOTES

Write any notes, insights or questions you have here so you can ponder or revisit at another time.

Chapter 14: The Bowls

Revelation 16:1-21

Each of us has to make a conscious decision to pursue God.

To not decide is still a decision.

It is a no-decision for God, by default.

READ

In your bible, read Revelation 16:1-21.

THINK

Think of your hometown, a favorite place or a place you know well. What does it look like after the pouring of the seven bowls?

DO

Looking in Revelation 16:1-21, complete the following questions and activities.

1. Read Revelation 16:4-5.

   · Who are "they" and "them"?

2. Who did not repent?

3. The dragon, the beast, and the false prophet have three unclean spirits come out of their mouths. Who are the unclean spirits? What do they do?

4. Where do the kings gather?

5. Complete the table.

	Where is the bowl poured?	What does it do?	What is the result or effect?
Bowl 1			
Bowl 2			
Bowl 3			
Bowl 4			
Bowl 5			
Bowl 6			

6. **Fill in the blank**

"It is _____.

7. What is *it?*

MY NOTES

Write any notes, insights or questions you have here so you can ponder or revisit at another time.

Chapter 15: Immoral Babylon

Revelation 17:1-18

You can understand more than you realize.

Read and see what you see.

Don't stop if something is hard to understand.

Just have faith and continue on.

(You are doing great, by the way, keep going!)

READ

In your bible, read Revelation 17:1-18.

THINK

Describe behaviors, thoughts and actions associated with immorality.

DO

Looking in Revelation 17:1-18, complete the following questions and activities.

1. What is the woman/great harlot sitting on?

2. What is the title on the woman's forehead?

3. Who are the 10 horns and what is their purpose?

4. What does the Lamb overcome?

5. Who is with the Lamb?

6. What is the woman's/great harlot's relationship with the kings of the earth?

7. Complete the table. Just read and list what you see for each entity. There may be more information on some entities than others.

The woman/the great harlot	The scarlet beast	The seven kings	The ten horns

MY NOTES

Write any notes, insights or questions you have here so you can ponder or revisit at another time.

Chapter 16: Fallen Babylon

Revelation 18:1-24

The next words are, *After this…*

After what? After Babylon is described in all her decay. There is a condemnation from heaven – Babylon is now a place of demons and prison for unclean spirits. It is a demonic spiritual realm.

Not good.

But the physical realm is not good either. It is fallen.

READ

In your bible, read Revelation 18:1-24.

THINK

Revelation 18:13: The NIV translation says two cargoes are *bodies and souls of men*. The NASB translation says *slaves and human lives*. Could this be a reference to human trafficking? Whether it is or not, please take a moment to pray for the victims of these crimes.

DO

Looking in Revelation 18:1-24, complete the following questions and activities.

1. Describe Babylon in Rev 18:1-3. Who is speaking?

2. Describe Babylon in Rev 18:4-5. Who is speaking?

3. List the cargoes of the merchants of the earth.

4. Who was led astray by "her" magic spell?

5. What was found in Babylon?

6. Complete the chart to describe the emotions and reactions to Babylon's destruction.

Who reacted	How did they react?
Kings of the earth	
Merchants of the earth	
Sea captains, passengers, sailors	

7. What benefit did the kings and merchants get from aligning with the woman, Babylon? (The answers are in Revelation 18)

Pause Button #4

Look how much you have studied! Revelation has 22 chapters, you have completed 18! I just knew you could do it! This is the last Pause Button; the next stop is the end of this first study.

1. What do you know from studying Revelation 14-18? Not necessarily understand, but what do you know or are aware of?

2. Did you gain an insight or a new perspective on something? If yes, what?

3. What did you learn?

Chapter 17: Christ Returns

Revelation 19:1-21

Another, *after this...*

What just happened? Babylon's destruction. Now, heaven weighs in and, it is spectacular! But there are consequences for those who go against God.

Remember – one line, two sides.

The beast and the false prophet are on one side of the line.

Jesus is on the other side of the line.

READ

In your bible, read Revelation 19:1-21.

THINK

What is the purpose of a wedding?

DO

Looking in Revelation 19:1-21, complete the following questions and activities.

1. The chapter begins with "After this/After these things." List *these things*.

2. What did God do?

3. What does the fine linen represent?

4. Who is blessed?

5. John falls down to worship the angel. What does the angel say to John, what is their relationship?

6. Heaven opened and what happened? List what you see in Revelation 19:11-16.

7. Who is thrown into the lake of fire and for how long?

8. How were the rest killed?

9. What is Jesus' weapon?

MY NOTES

Write any notes, insights or questions you have here so you can ponder or revisit at another time.

Chapter 18: One Thousand Years

Revelation 20:1-15

1,000 years.

The lake of fire.

The second death.

The Book of Life.

READ

In your bible, read Revelation 20:1-15.

THINK

Two choices, one decision. Is it eternity with Jesus in heaven, or in the lake of fire with the devil? What do you believe about these two choices?

DO

Looking in Revelation 20:1-15, complete the following questions and activities.

1. Who is the dragon?

2. What happens to him?

3. What/who reigns with Christ during the 1,000 years? (The 1,000 years is also known as the Millennium)

4. Who is part of the first resurrection?

5. What happens at the end of the 1,000 years?

6. Where is the devil's final destination? Who is already there?

7. What book(s) judged the dead according to what they had done?

8. What is the second death?

9. What happens if someone's name is not written in the book of life?

10. Describe the Great White Throne – what is happening?

MY NOTES

Write any notes, insights or questions you have here so you can ponder or revisit at another time.

Chapter 19: Life Eternal

Revelation 21:1-22:6

"I am making everything new!" – God (Rev 21:5)

READ

In your bible, read Revelation 21:1-22:6.

THINK

How does your name get into the Lamb's Book of Life?

DO

Looking in Revelation 21:1-22:6, complete the following questions and activities.

1. What happened to the first heaven and the first earth?

2. Where is the Holy City, New Jerusalem?

3. Where is the dwelling of God and who is with him?

4. What will God do?

5. What is the promise to those who overcome?

6. Make a list of those who are in the lake of fire.

7. How does the city get its light?

8. Is there night and day?

9. Who will enter New Jerusalem?

10. Who will not live in New Jerusalem?

11. Read Revelation 19:9, Revelation 21:5 and Revelation 22:6. What do *"these words"* have in common?

12. Where are those who accept and follow Christ?

13. Where are those who reject, or never accept, who God and Christ are?

MY NOTES

Write any notes, insights or questions you have here so you can ponder or revisit at another time.

Chapter 20: Last Words

Revelation 22: 7-21

"Blessed is he who keeps the words of the prophecy written in this book."

(Rev 22:7)

READ

In your bible, read Revelation 22:7-21.

THINK

The angel's admonishment to John is to worship God. Do you find it easier to worship people or things instead of God? Why or why not?

DO

Looking in Revelation 22:7-21, complete the following questions and activities.

1. List those who are inside the city and those outside the city.

Inside the city	Outside the city

2. What are the two warnings?

3. What are the consequences of not obeying the warnings?

4. When is Jesus coming back?

5. Who will be blessed and why?

6. Read Revelation 1:1-8. What does this passage mean to you now after studying the entire book of Revelation?

MY NOTES

Write any notes, insights or questions you have here so you can ponder or revisit at another time.

Take a Big Deep Breath

Well done on finishing this study of Revelation! Now, take some time to answer these questions to help you see what you gained from this study. Excellent work and perseverance!

1. What do you know from studying the book of Revelation? Not necessarily understand, but what do you know or are aware of?

2. What are the main insights or perspectives you gained from this study?

3. Read over your *My Notes* in each chapter and the *Pause Button* sections. Write your observations here.

4. What is the book of Revelation about? Support your answer with scripture.

5. The previous question you answered at the beginning of the book. Go back to the beginning of this book and look at your answer. Compare your first answer with the one you just wrote. Write your observations on your two answers — what is different, changed, the same?

6. These are the three questions posed at the beginning of this guide. Think about each one and give an answer based on what you studied in Revelation.

·   Is Revelation literal or symbolic?

·   Is Revelation in chronological order?

·   Is Revelation in the past, in the present or in the future?

NEXT STEPS

There is more to learn and uncover, here are some ideas for your next steps.

- Look at bible commentaries to gain insight from another's interpretation. Read more than one commentary, so you get more than one perspective. Many commentaries are similar, yet each one has its own style.

- Begin *The Second Study* in this guide. You completed *The First Study*, so I know you can complete *The Second Study*!

- Read the next two chapters in this guide that are about Jesus

The Choice for Jesus

It is all about Jesus. It is all about choice – Jesus or no Jesus. It is about two destinations for our eternity. To spend it with Jesus in heaven or to spend it in the lake of fire with the devil.

We often don't like the black and white of things. It is more comfortable to live in the gray zone. The gray zone, where no decisions are required. The gray zone, where you live a good life, are a good person, do good things, work hard and you are an unbeliever. Living life in the gray zone doesn't get you into heaven, belief does. Belief requires a decision, a mindset. A black or white choice.

Yes, you can have a healthy belief in yourself. But, is your motivation for yourself? "I am good because of what I do" or is the motivation, "God is good, and I want to do good because of him" It is a choice. And at times, it is a struggle.

As you have learned, God is the one who holds the key to our eternity. Not in a way that we have to flounder and figure it out. He has a well-designed and orderly plan that shows His mercy by going to extremes to get our attention.

The extreme measure in the form of Jesus Christ. Who took on human form and life, complete with trouble and temptation.

Jesus overcame trouble and temptation. He suffered and died on a cross to be our escape plan from God's wrath. Jesus *is* the plan to bring us into eternity with God, not separated from God.

Jesus comes back to earth to claim his own; to those who make a choice to follow him. Is Jesus coming back for you?

Making the Choice for Jesus

Jesus did not die just to give us peace and a purpose in life;
He died to save us from the wrath of God.

– Jerry Bridges

Forgiven

Forgiven means that God does not hold your past against you. God forgives you when you place your faith in Christ. God forgives your wrongs whatever they are when you put your faith in Christ.

Therefore, there is now no condemnation for those who are in Christ Jesus.
(Romans 8:1)

What do you want God to forgive you for? You can ask forgiveness for anything when it comes to God. If you mean it. We have a big, living God. Ask Him.

Repent

Repent means to turn back, away from behavior that is not in line with God. You want to change. Believing in Christ turns you toward God.

That if you confess with your mouth Jesus as Lord, and believe in your heart that God raised Him from the dead, you will be saved. (Romans 10:9)

What do you want to confess? What do you want to change? Even if the change seems impossible, it is not impossible for God. We have a big, living God. Ask him to help you change.

Saved

Saved means you are not subject to God's wrath. You just read about God's wrath. Through your faith in Jesus Christ, God will save you from his wrath.

Jesus said to him, I am the way, and the truth, and the life;
no one comes to the Father but through Me. (John 14:6)

There is no work you can do to save you. Doing good things will not save you, being a nice person does not save you. Only faith in Christ saves you.

Therefore if anyone is in Christ, he is a new creature:
the old things passed away; behold, new things have come. (2 Corinthians 5:17)

What do you need to be saved from? Ask God to save you. If you mean it in your heart, He will save you. We have a big, living God. Ask Him.

Living with Christ

Living with Christ does not mean life is without trouble. It doesn't mean you don't make mistakes. It does mean you have strength in Christ to get through what it is you need to get through. If things seem like they are going sideways in your life whether for a season or a moment, keep in mind this verse:

"I can do all things in Christ who strengthens me."
(Philippians 4:13)

Amen!

The
Second
Study

The More You Know, The More You Know

"No short cut exists for a deeper spiritual life.
The man who would know God must give time to Him."

— AW Tozer

"Knowledge is power."

Seems true. The more you know, the more you know, and with that can come a sense of power.

The danger comes when a person takes what she knows and lauds it over others who do not know. Puffed up knowledge is pride, not a good thing. Puffed up knowledge can be a source of problems within the realm of Bible study.

So here is a different slant. *With knowledge comes responsibility.* Responsibility attached to knowledge becomes a thing to do conscientiously.

You must share, act or initiate change because of what you know.

Knowledge gleaned from the bible is meant to be shared, with gentleness, for another's benefit.

But in your hearts revere Christ as Lord. Always be prepared to give
an answer to everyone who asks you to give the reason for the hope
that you have. But do this with gentleness and respect, keeping a clear
conscience, so that those who speak maliciously against your good
behavior in Christ may be ashamed of their slander.
1 Peter 3:15-16 (NIV)

Keep this sense of responsibility in mind as you take another run through Revelation. We are all responsible for what we know. What will you do with what you know?

If we understand what lies ahead for those who do not know Christ,
there will be a sense of urgency in our witness.

– David Jeremiah

What You Will Do – The Second Study

Why Take a Second Look?

As you now know, there is much to digest in Revelation. In addition to the questions and activities you did in *The First Study*, going through it a second time gives you more insight. But now, we want to do different things to see different facets of this book. We want to,

- Explore the words we read, their meaning, and the context they are used.
- Substantiate the message by looking in other parts of the bible.
- Build on what we know from *The First Study* with reflective questions and activities.

These activities take time, thought and research. But in doing so, you move from awareness of Revelation's message to understanding Revelation's message.

Stick with it; you will be glad you did.

Word Studies

A word study shows us the original meaning of the word and its intent. It helps provide the context of its use in a verse. What you learn can be a rich discovery and also surprising. Word studies are best done with a word-for-word translation (NASB) or thought-for-thought translation (NIV). It will be difficult using a paraphrase like The Message.

What you need to do a word study is a concordance. A concordance lists words found in the Bible. I recommend one of these, depending on the Bible translation you use.

- *The NIV Exhaustive Bible Concordance, Third Edition* (available in print only as of this writing). Use this with the NIV Bible.

· *The Strong's Exhaustive Concordance* (available in print, online, and with some bible apps). There are two versions, one for the NASB Bible and another for the King James Bible.

Let's do a word study together using *The NIV Exhaustive Bible Concordance, Third Edition*. Let's study the word "revelation" in Revelation 1:1.

The **revelation** *from Jesus Christ,*
which God gave him to show his servants what must soon take place.

First, what is your definition of revelation when you read it in this verse? Write your answer here.

Now, let's see what *The NIV Exhaustive Bible Concordance, Third Edition* says about the word *revelation* in this verse.

Revelation - Reveal; to make information known with an implication that the information can be understood. To God, making information known, especially to His close associates.

Let's put this definition into the verse.

The revelation **(information known that can be understood; information from God especially to His close associates)** *from Jesus Christ, which God gave him to show his servants what must soon take place.*

Look back at your definition – how does it match up? For me, the word revelation means to reveal or gain insight into something not previously thought of. Like *"Aha, this thought just came to me!"* While this may be a passable definition, it is not what the original meaning is in this text.

Its original meaning conveys not only the idea of information to be known, but also this information comes from God, to be known. In this verse, this revelation from Jesus via God is one that God wants us to know about. Right from the beginning, God is telling us He wants us to know.

See how that brings a richer meaning to the verse?

Looking at words and what they mean in their original form and in context gives depth and richness to the bible. The modern-day meaning of a word may be different, so to read the original intent gives you the best understanding.

Doing word studies separates you from many people who study the bible. You are learning on your own and not letting someone else tell you what it means.

Cross-Referencing Verses

Researching what the bible says about a topic, event or person beyond one verse is mind-expanding. Here is a practice cross-referencing activity on two people in the bible – Priscilla and Aquila. This is a verse to start with, Acts 18:1-3.

After this, Paul left Athens and went to Corinth. There he met a Jew named Aquila, a native of Pontus, who had recently come from Italy with his wife Priscilla, because Claudius had ordered all Jews to leave Rome. Paul went to see them, and because he was a tentmaker as they were, he stayed and worked with them.

Look up the following verses and write what you learn about Aquila and Priscilla.

Acts 18:18-19; 24-26

Romans 16:3

1 Corinthians 16:19

2 Timothy 4:19

Summarize what you know about Priscilla and Aquila.

See how cross-referencing is mind-expanding?

References and Helps

Here are some references and helps for your study.

· *The NIV Exhaustive Bible Concordance, Third Edition* (available in print only as of this writing). Use this with the NIV Bible.
· *The Strong's Exhaustive Concordance* (available in print, online, and with some bible apps). There are two versions, one for the NASB Bible and another for the King James Bible.
· Online – A good overall resource is *biblestudytools.com.* There are numerous bible and bible study apps. Check your app store to see what is available to you. You can find apps with bibles (various translations), concordances, bible dictionaries along with other bible study helps.

The Bible is for Everyone

Remember, the Bible is for all of us to read and discern on our own. It is not a super-secret book only for a select few. It is for you.

By the way – congratulations on your decision to complete this second study! Let's get started!

Chapter 1-2: The Holy Trinity - God, Jesus, and the Holy Spirit

Revelation 1:1-20

It was the whole Trinity, which at the beginning of creation said, "Let us make man." It was the whole Trinity again, which at the beginning of the Gospel seemed to say, "Let us save man."

– J. C. Ryle

READ

In your bible, read Revelation 1:1-20.

THINK

Read the above quote. What do you know about the Trinity?

DO

Looking in Revelation 1:1-20, complete the following questions and activities.

Word Studies

Use a concordance to look up these words and write the definitions here.

1. Revelation (Rev 1:1)

    Put the definition into the verse.

    The revelation (_____) of Jesus Christ...

2. Servants (Rev 1:2)

    Put the definition into the verse.

    ...to show his servants _____ what must soon take place.

3. Testifies (Rev 1:2)

    People who follow Christ and share their story of how they began to follow him are said to give their testimony. Based on the definition of testimony, what does this mean? What do they share?

4. Alpha and Omega (Rev 1:8)

Cross – References

Look up these bible verses to learn more about each word or topic. Write the verses down here.

5. God (Rev 1:1)
   a. Genesis 1:1

   b. John 4:24

   c. Acts 10:34

   d. Galatians 6:7-8

e. 1John 4:9

6. Jesus (Rev 1:5)
   a. Matthew 9:12-13

   b. John 1:29

   c. John 3:16-18

   d. Acts 2:32-33

7. Holy Spirit
    a. John 14:16-17, 26

    b. Romans 5:5

    c. 2 Corinthians 13:14

8. Write a description for each entity based on what you found in your cross-references.

	Description based on scripture
God	
Jesus	
Holy Spirit	

Chapter 2-2: Hear

Revelation 2:1-29

*We often miss hearing God's voice simply because
we aren't paying attention.*

– Rick Warren

READ

In your bible, read Revelation 2:1-29.

THINK

Read the above quote. How do you pay attention so you can hear God's voice?

DO

Looking in Revelation 2:1-29, complete the following questions and activities.

Word Studies

Use a concordance to look up these words and write the definitions here.

1. Repent (Rev 2:5)

   Is there anything you want to repent of? If yes, what and why?

2. Persecution (Rev 2:10)

3. Hear (Rev 2:7, 11, 17)

   People will say "I heard from God" to explain a decision or direction they took in their life. What are your thoughts about that? Have you ever heard from God? If yes, what were the circumstances? If no, do you believe it is possible to hear from God? Why?

Cross – References

Look up these bible verses to learn more about each word or topic. Write the verses here.

4. Tree of life (Rev 2:7)
    a. Genesis 2:8-9

    b. Genesis 3:22-24

Where is the tree of life located? What does it do?

5. Satan (Rev 2:9)
    a. Romans 16:20

    b. 2 Corinthians 11:14-15

    c. Revelation 12:7-9

d. 1 John 3:8

Write a sentence or two describing Satan and his followers.

What is another name for Satan?

Who is Satan's enemy?

6. Jezebel (Rev 2:20)
   a. 1 Kings 16:31

Who did she marry?

What was her position or title?

b. 1 Kings 18:4

Who did she have killed?

7. Re-read Revelation 2:20-22.

   What is the situation?

   How does this relate to the verses you looked up in 1ˢᵗ and 2ⁿᵈ Kings? Why do you think Jesus uses the name Jezebel in these verses?

Chapter 3-2: Overcome

Revelation 3:1-22

Nothing paralyzes our lives like the attitude that things can never change. We need to remind ourselves that God can change things. Outlook determines outcome. If we see only the problems, we will be defeated: but if we see possibilities in the problems, we can have victory.

— Warren Wiersbe

READ

In your bible, read Revelation 3:1-22.

THINK

Read the above quote. How can you remind yourself to see God and possibilities in your problems?

DO

Looking in Revelation 3:1-22, complete the following questions and activities.

Word Studies

Use a concordance to look up these words and write the definitions here.

1. Deeds (Rev 3:2)

   Put the definition into the verse.

   These are the words of him who holds the seven Spirits of God and the seven stars. I know your deeds (_____); you have a reputation of being alive but you are dead.

2. Complete the chart for each church letter.

	Ephesus	Smyrna	Pergamum	Thyatira
Praise				
Reprimand				
Command				
Consequence				
Warning				
Promise				

	Sardis	Philadelphi	Laodicea
Praise			
Reprimand			
Command			
Consequence			
Warning			
Promise			

3. Write a summary statement for the seven letters.

Pause Button #1

This is different isn't it? Many people do not take time to study the bible in this way, but you are and I hope you are seeing that it is worth it! Don't rush, be deliberate and thoughtful – pray to God when you have questions or are convicted of something. Review your work in *The First Study,* chapters 1-3 in this book, and do the following.

1. Write anything that now is clearer or is a new insight.

2. What did you learn from doing the word studies and cross referencing?

3. What questions do you have?

Chapter 4-2: Worship

Revelation 4:1-5:14

For worship is, essentially, the reverse of sin. Sin began (and begins) when we succumb to the temptation, "You shall be as gods." We make ourselves the center of the universe and dethrone God. By contrast, worship is giving God His time worth; it is acknowledging Him to be the Lord of all things, and the Lord of everything in our lives. He is, indeed, the Most High God.

– Sinclair Ferguson

READ

In your bible, read Revelation 4:1-5:14.

THINK

Read the above quote. What is a situation where you make (or have made) yourself the center of the universe and ignore God?

DO

Looking in Revelation 4:1-5:14, complete the following questions and activities.

Questions

1. Where is the scroll? (Rev 5:1)

2. Describe the scroll.

3. What is the problem? (Rev 5:2-3)

4. What is John's reaction to the problem? (Rev 5:4)

5. How is the problem solved? (Rev 5:5)

Cross – References

Look up these bible verses to learn more about each word or topic.

6. Redeemed (Rev 5:9)
   a. 1 Peter 1:17-19

   b. 1 Corinthians 6:20

   How are you redeemed?

   Who is the Lamb without blemish?

7. John (Rev 5:12)

    a. John 1:29

       What does John testify to?

    b. John 1:35-36

       What does John say to Jesus?

8. Draw Revelation 5:6-8.

Chapter 5-2: Destruction

Revelation 6:1-17

Pride is the parent of destruction;
pride eats the mind and the heart and soul alive.

– Anne Rice

READ

In your bible, read Revelation 6:1-17.

THINK

Read the above quote. What does it mean that, *"pride eats the mind and the heart and soul alive"?*

DO

Looking in Revelation 6:1-17, complete the following questions and activities.

Word Studies

Use a concordance to look up these words and write the definitions here.

1. Seal (Rev 6:1)

Who is the only one who can break the seal in the book?

2. Souls (Rev 6:9)

You looked at the word *testimony* in Chapter 1-2 in this guide. What did these souls do? Why were they slain?

3. Judge (Rev 6:10)

Describe a time you were judged for your actions.

4. Wrath (Rev 6:16-17)

Describe a person who is displaying wrath.

Cross – References

Look up these bible verses to learn more about each word or topic.

5. Wrath (Rev 6:16-17)
   a. John 3:36

   b. Romans 1:18

   c. Romans 5:9

   d. 1 Thessalonians 5:9

6. Relying on your cross reference research for *wrath*, describe the following from Revelation 6:16:

   a. What is the wrath of the Lamb?

   b. What is the great day of wrath?

   c. Who is hiding from this wrath?

7. A common phrase in Christianity is *"I am saved by Jesus."* Given what you have learned from cross-referencing, what does this phrase mean?

8. Complete the chart for the seven seals.

Seal	Event(s)	Consequence(s)
1		
2		
3		
4		
5		
6		
7		

9. Write a summary statement for the seven seals.

Chapter 6-2: Salvation

Revelation 7:1-17

A world of nice people, content in their own niceness, looking no further, turned away from God, would be just as desperately in need of salvation as a miserable world – and might be even more difficult to save.

– C. S. Lewis

READ

In your bible, read Revelation 7: 1-17.

THINK

Read the above quote. We might think bad people need God, not nice people. But, people who turn away from God, even the nice ones, need him too. Why is being nice not enough to be in good standing with God?

DO

Looking in Revelation 7: 1-17, complete the following questions and activities.

Word Studies

Use a concordance to look up these words and write the definitions here.

1. Salvation (Rev 7:10)

   Put the definition into the verse.

   Salvation (_____) belongs to our

   God, who sits on the throne, and to the Lamb.

2. Tribulation (Rev 7:14)

   "The tribulation" is commonly used to describe the end times. What is your definition or description of the tribulation?

Questions

3. Who are the 144,000? (Rev 7:4)

4. Where do those in the white robes come from? (Rev 7:13)

Cross — References

Look up these bible verses to learn more about each word or topic.

5. Blood of the Lamb/of Christ (Rev 7:14)
   a. Leviticus 14:25

      What type of offering is given?

   b. 1 Peter 1:18-21

   c. Revelation 1:4-6

      What does the blood of the Lamb, this offering, represent?

6. Great tribulation/distress (Rev 7:14)

    a. Matthew 24:12-27

    What has to happen and then the end will come?

    How is this great distress/tribulation described? (Matthew 24:21)

    What is Jesus' warning about in Matthew 24:23-26?

7. Can you think of a situation where a person(s) has shed their blood for another as a sacrifice?

Activity

8. Draw verses Revelation 7:1-3

9. What is being prevented?

10. What has to happen before harm comes to the land and the sea?

Chapter 7-2: Prayer

Revelation 8:1-9:21

God tolerates even our stammering, and pardons our ignorance whenever something inadvertently escapes us – as, indeed, without this mercy there would be no freedom to pray.

– John Calvin

READ

In your bible, read Revelation 8:1-9:21.

THINK

Read the above quote. What do you relate to? Well articulated prayer or stammering and stuttering prayer? Write a prayer just off the top of your head, don't edit, and don't worry about grammar or spelling. Just write what is on your heart and mind. Then, pray your prayer.

DO

Looking in Revelation 8:1-9:21, complete the following questions and activities.

Word Studies

Use a concordance to look up these words and write the definitions here.

1. Prayer (Rev 8:3-4)

   What is your definition of prayer?

2. Worship (Revelation 9:20)

   What is the focus of your worship?

   Is this a living or non-living entity?

   Describe how this entity has the power to help, encourage, and guide the way you live.

3. Idols (Revelation 9:20)

   What can idols not do?

Cross – References

4. Read Isaiah 44. List what you learn about God and those who make idols.

God/the Lord	Those who make idols

5. Who has more power when you worship them? God or an idol?

6. Who is the rest of mankind worshipping? (Rev 9:20)

Pause Button #2

Great work getting to this point in your Revelation study! Did the Isaiah 44 mini-study expand your knowledge of God and of idols? Review your work in *The First Study*, chapters 4-7 in this book, and do the following.

1. Write anything the either became clearer or a new insight after completing these second study activities.

2. What did you learn from doing the word studies and cross referencing?

3. Did you answer any of the questions from the first study?

Chapter 8-2: Prophecy

Revelation 10:1-11

Prophecy is an intercept from the mind of an all-knowing and all-seeing and all-powerful God.

— Joel Rosenberg

READ

In your bible, read Revelation 10:1-11.

THINK

Read the above quote. Look up the word *intercept* in a dictionary. What is this quote saying about God communicating with us?

DO

Looking in Revelation 10:1-11, complete the following questions and activities.

Word Studies

Use a concordance to look up these words and write the definitions here.

1. Mystery (Rev 10:7)

2. Prophesy (Rev 10:11)

3. Using the verses listed under each word, compare these three words. Review your work in Chapter 1-2 in this guide for the word *revelation*.

	Mystery Revelation 10:17	Prophesy Revelation 10:11	Revelation Revelation 1:1
Description			
What are the differences between these words?			
How are these differences important?			

4. Look up 2 Peter 1:20-21.

   a. Fill in the blanks.

   Above all, you must understand that_____prophecy of

   Scripture came about by the prophet's own interpretation of things.

   For prophecy _____had its origin in the human will, but

   prophets, though human, _____ _____ _____ as they were

   carried along by the Holy Spirit.

   b. Who is the only originator of prophecy?

Chapter 9-2: Resurrection

Revelation 11:1-19

*Our Lord has written the promise of resurrection, not in books alone
but in every leaf in springtime.*

— Martin Luther

READ

In your bible, read Revelation 11:1-19.

THINK

Read the above quote. Take a couple of minutes to write down some things you associate with springtime. Then, look over your list and circle the things that symbolize the promise of rebirth or newness. Pick one of these and write a couple of sentences, or longer if you want, on how this symbolizes newness and rebirth to you.

DO

Looking in Revelation 11:1-19, complete the following questions and activities.

Cross – References

Look up these bible verses to learn more about each word or topic.

1. Ark of His Covenant/Ark of the Covenant

    a. Exodus 25:1-9

        Where will God dwell?

        Who will he dwell with?

    b. Exodus 25:21-25

        What will go in the ark?

2. The Ark and God's Power

    a. Joshua 3

        How does God's power show through the ark?

3. The Ark and God's Presence

   a. Leviticus 16:1-2

      How does God appear?

      Where does God appear?

   b. Numbers 10:33-36

      Where is the ark?

      How does the Lord appear?

4. Read 2 Chronicles 35:1-4. This is the last mention of the Ark in the Old Testament.

   Where is the ark?

5. Describe or draw what happens after the seventh trumpet sounds. (Rev 11:15-19)

Where is the ark?

Where is God?

What happens? Is this scene powerful or meek?

6. What did you learn about the seven trumpets? Complete the chart.

Trumpet	Event(s)	Consequence(s)
1		
2		
3		
4		
5		
6		
7		

7. Write a summary statement for the seven trumpets. Describe or draw what happens after the seventh trumpet sounds.

Chapter 10-2: Battles

Revelation 12:1-17

There are many inacceptable reasons for war. Imperialism. Financial gain. Religion. Family feuds. Racial arrogance. There are many unacceptable motives for war. But there is one time when war is condoned and used by God: wickedness.

— Max Lucado

READ

In your bible, read Revelation 12:1-17.

THINK

Read the above quote. What do you believe are mankind's top three reasons for war? They do not need to be ones mentioned in the quote. Give reasons for why you believe this.

DO

Looking in Revelation 12:1-17, complete the following questions and activities.

Word Studies

Use a concordance to look up this word and write the definition here.

1. Sign (Rev 12:1,3)

    Using the definition, how do you characterize the signs in verses 12:1 and 3?

Questions

Answer the following questions from Revelation 12.

2. Where is the dragon? List all citations.

3. What is the dragon doing on earth?

4. Who is Michael? Look up the following verses.

    a. Daniel 10:13, 21

    b. Jude 9

    c. Revelation 12:7

5. Where is Michael in Revelation 12? List all citations.

6. Where does the war between the dragon and Michael take place?

7. What is the outcome of this war?

Chapter 11-2: The Unholy Trinity:
Satan, the Beast and the False Prophet

Revelation 13:1-18

There is a Holy Trinity,
and there is likewise a Trinity of Evil.

– A.W. Pink

READ

In your bible, read Revelation 13:1-18.

THINK

Read the above quote. Describe evil.

DO

Looking in Revelation 13:1-18, complete the following questions and activities.

Word Studies

Use a concordance to look up these words and write the definitions here.

1. Authority (Rev 13:2,4,7,12)

    Put the definition into the verse.

    The dragon gives the beast his power and his throne and great authority (_____

    _____).

    How did the first beast use this authority?

    The 2ⁿᵈ beast exercised all the authority (_____) of

    the first beast on his behalf.

    How does the second beast use his authority?

2. Blaspheme (Rev 13:6)

Who did the beast blaspheme?

Cross – References

Look up these bible verses to learn more about each word or topic.

3.   Those who live on the earth/inhabitants of the earth (Rev 13:14)

a.   Revelation 3:10

What is going to happen to them?

b.   Revelation 8:13

What is the warning to them?

What happens after the warning? (Read Rev 9; Rev 11:15-19)

4. Contrast God and the dragon. Complete the chart by looking up the verses, writing them here, and then answering the questions.

God	The dragon/Satan
Revelation 1:1-2	Revelation 12:7-9
Revelation 4:1-8	Revelation 13:1

Where is God?

Where is Satan?

What is the contrast between God and Satan?

5. Contrast Jesus and the first beast. Complete the chart by looking up the verses, writing them here, and then answering the questions.

Jesus/Lamb	The first beast
Revelation 5:1-8	Revelation 13:1-4

Where does Jesus come from to fulfill his mission?

Where does the best come out of to fulfill his mission?

What is the contrast between the Jesus and the first beast?

Who worships Jesus? Where are they?

Who worships the beast? Where are they?

6. Contrast the Holy Spirit and the second beast. Complete the chart by looking up the verses, writing them here, and then answering the questions.

Holy Spirit	The second beast
John 14:15-17, 26	Revelation 13:11-15

Where does the Holy Spirit come from?

Who does the Holy Spirit help? Who is he for?

Where does the second beast come from?

Who does the second beast deceive and why?

What is the contrast between the Holy Spirit and the second beast?

Pause Button #3

Remember, Revelation 1:1 – God wants us to know what this revelation is, but it is also in his time, not all at once. Do not worry if you are feeling confused or overwhelmed, getting this far in your study is great! Keep going.

Review your work in *The First Study*, chapters 8-11 in this book, and do the following

1. Write anything the either became clearer or a new insight after completing these second study activities.

2. Did you answer any questions you had from the first study? If yes, what?

3. What did you learn from doing the word studies and cross referencing?

Chapter 12-2: Wrath

Revelation 14:1-20

The wrath of God is a way of saying that I have been living in a way that is contrary to the love that is God. Anyone who begins to live and grow away from God, who lives away from what is good, is turning his life towards wrath.

— Pope Benedict XVI

READ

In your bible, read Revelation 14:1-20.

THINK

Read the above quote. How is worshipping someone or something other than God a direction towards God's wrath?

DO

Looking in Revelation 14:1-20, complete the following questions and activities.

Exploring the word *wrath*.

1. Revelation 14:10 - *Wrath* of God

    Definition: *Feeling and expression of strong displeasure and hostility.* This word is different than wrath used in Revelation 14:19.

2. Revelation 14:19 - Great winepress of God's *wrath*

    Definition: *A state of intense displeasure; the anger of God is due to moral offense and a focus on righteous judgment.*

3. What is the result of the first sickle?

4. What is the result of the second sickle?

5. What happens to the gathered grapes?

6. Review the definitions at the top of the page. What is the difference between the action/result of the first sickle and the action/result of the second sickle?

Cross – References

Look up the bible verses to learn more about each word or topic.

7. My [God] Name / for My [God] Name's sake

    a. Isaiah 42:8

    b. Ezekiel 20:44

    c. Ezekiel 36:22

8. Given what you just researched, why does God's wrath and discipline need to happen?

9. What if God let sin, and anti-God behavior happen without consequence? What would that say about his trustworthiness and honor?

10. Have you ever been in a situation that you had to defend your honor, your name? If yes, what was the circumstance? If no, can you think of a situation or person who had to defend their name and honor?

11. Why is it important to us to defend our name and honor?

Chapter 13-2: Glory

Revelation 15:1-8

It would seem that unless we see through and beyond the physical, we shall not even see the physical as we ought to see it: as the very vehicle for the glory of God.

– Elisabeth Elliot

READ

In your bible, read Revelation 15:1-8.

THINK

Read the above quote. Look around where you are. Make a list of physical things that are a vehicle for the glory of God. Add other physical things that are not in your sight which represents the glory of God.

DO

Looking in Revelation 15:1-8, complete the following questions and activities.

Word Studies

Use a concordance to look up these words and write the definitions here.

1. Plague (Rev 15:1)

2. Glory (Rev 15:8)

Put the definition into the verse.

And the temple was filled with the smoke from the glory (_____

_____) of God and from his power...

Questions

Answer the following questions, using what you have learned in the bible.

3. Who is in heaven? (Rev 15:1-2)

4. What did God give them? (Rev 15:1-2)

5. What are God's qualities? Make a list. (Rev 15:3-4)

6. The people on earth who worship the image of the beast can look at what they are worshipping. The image. Believers in Christ worship Christ, unseen. What does it take to believe in Christ unseen? If you do not believe in Christ, what do you need to believe in him?

7. Draw Revelation 15:5-8. Write on your drawing what the seven angels are wearing.

Chapter 14-2: Judgment

Revelation 16:1-21

Better to confess Christ 1,000 times now and be despised by men,
than be disowned by Christ before God in the Day of Judgment.

– J.C. Ryle

READ

In your bible, read Revelation 16:1-21.

THINK

Read the above quote. Despised is a strong word choice. Despised is to be disdained, detested, or loathed. Why are people who follow Christ, who look to him for guidance and strength, despised by people who ignore or reject him? Why is that? Why the strong emotion?

DO

Looking in Revelation 16:1-21, complete the following questions and activities.

Cross – References

Look up the bible verses to learn more about each word or topic.

1. Wicked
   a. Proverbs 11:21

2. Evil
   a. Romans 2:5-8

3. Sinful nature
   a. Galatians 5:19-21

4. Read Romans 1:18-32.

   a. What is God's response to those who reject him?

   b. What are people's actions as they move away from God's ways?

5. Read Romans 1:32. What is being encouraged? Who is doing the encouraging?

6. Review your cross-reference work in Chapter 12-2 in this guide on why God defends his name.

   a. Why is it that God cannot allow sin and must defend His name?

   b. What did you find out about God-ordained destruction and his wrath?

7. Review the six bowls and list the places/people/things the bowls were poured on.

	Where/who/what was the bowl poured on?	What is the result?
Bowl 1		
Bowl 2		
Bowl 3		
Bowl 4		
Bowl 5		
Bowl 6		
Bowl 7		

8. Write a summary statement for the seven bowls.

Chapter 15-2: Satan

Revelation 17:1-18

Satan's aim is to destroy our joy and trust and delight in God, and to make God look worthless in the world's eyes. Every time someone forsakes God for the world, gets angry at God when part of the world is taken away from them, they highlight the world as valuable...and every time someone stays with God, when the world is taken away, and praises God, they highlight the value and glory of God.

– John Piper

READ

In your bible, read Revelation 17:1-18.

THINK

Read the above quote. Describe what you give value to, God or the world?

DO

Looking in Revelation 17:1-18, complete the following questions and activities.

Word Studies

Use a concordance to look up these words and write the definitions here.

1. Prostitute (Rev 17:1)

2. Adultery (Rev 17:2)

3. Intoxicated (Rev 17:2)

4. Filth (Rev 17:4)

5. Abominable (Rev 17:5)

Questions

6. Read Revelation 17:1-5 with these definitions in mind. Then, describe Babylon the Great's moral and spiritual health.

7. Draw verses Revelation 17:3-7. Then, list on your drawing the meaning of the seven heads and the ten horns in Revelation 17:8-14. Who is the woman? How does she come to ruin?

Chapter 16-2: Mourn

Revelation 18:1-24

Man's inhumanity to man makes countless thousands mourn.

– Robert Burns

READ

In your bible, read Revelation 18:1-24.

THINK

Read the above quote. Why are people inhumane to others? How does this happen?

DO

Looking in Revelation 18:1-24, complete the following questions and activities.

Word Studies

Use a concordance to look up these words and write the definitions here.

1. Mourning (Rev 18:9)

   Who is mourning? Why?

Questions

2. What are the cargoes no longer purchased? (Rev 18:11-13)

3. Who are the people, skills, trades, no longer? (Rev 18:21-22)

4. What was found in Babylon? (Rev 18:24)

5. You are in Babylon walking the streets. What do you see?

6. What would you mourn the most, if anything?

Pause Button #4

You are studying the bible in a way that many do not do. Particularly with the book of Revelation. Not everything may make sense, but as you continue to read and study the bible, you will gain insights on what you are studying now. No one ever gets it all at once. Keep going!

Review your work in *The First Study*, chapters 12-16 in this book, and do the following.

1. Write anything the either became clearer or a new insight after completing these second study activities.

2. What did you learn from doing the word studies and cross referencing?

3. The image or visual that has made the biggest impact on me is...

Chapter 17-2: Testimony

Revelation 19:1-21

Yes, let God be the Judge. Your job today is to be a witness.

— Warren Wiersbe

READ

In your bible, read Revelation 19:1-21.

THINK

Read the above quote. How is your job as a witness for Christ going? What is going well? Is there something you want to get better at?

DO

Looking in Revelation 19:1-21, complete the following questions and activities.

Word Studies

Use a concordance to look up these words and write the definitions here.

1. Testimony (Rev 19:10)

    Put the definition into the verse.

    For the testimony (_____) of

    Jesus is the spirit of prophecy.

Cross – References

Look up the bible verses to learn more about each word or topic.

2. Testimony (Rev 19:10)
    a. Rev 6:9

    What happened because of their witness to the word of God?

3. Faithful and True (Rev 19:11)

    a. Revelation 3:19

    Who is this?

4. a sharp sword (Rev 19:15)
   a. Ephesians 6:17

   b. Hebrews 4:12

   c. Revelation 1:16

      What is this sharp sword?

5. Read Revelation 19:8 and 19:14.

   What does the fine linen represent?

   Who is wearing the fine linen?

   What makes up the armies in heaven with Jesus?

6. A wedding reception celebrates the union of marriage. What does the Great Supper of the Lamb acknowledge?

7. Draw Revelation 19:11-1. Include the words KING of KINGS and LORD of LORDS on your drawing.

Chapter 18-2: Perish

Revelation 20:1-15

For God so loved the world that he gave his one and only Son, that whoever believes in him shall not perish but have eternal life. For God did not send his Son into the world to condemn the world, but to save the world through him.

— John 3:16-17

READ

In your bible, read Revelation 20:1-15.

THINK

Read the above bible verse. Do you believe what it says? Why or why not?

DO

Looking in Revelation 20:1-15, complete the following questions and activities.

Cross – References

Look up the bible verses to learn more about each word or topic.

1. Perish

    a. 2 Peter 3:9

        What is God's will for people?

    b. Luke 13:1-8

        Does this say some people are better or more deserving than others to be saved from destruction?

A Study of Books

Look up these bible verses to learn more about each word or topic. Write the verses down here.

2. Read these *books of life* references in these verses.

    a. Revelation 3:4-5

        What will never happen to those who walk with Jesus?

b. Revelation 13:8

Whose names are not written in *the book of life*?

c. Exodus 32:33

d. Psalm 69:28

How can your name be blotted out of the book of life?

e. Revelation 20:15

What happens if your name is not in *the book of life*?

3. Lamb's book of life
    a. Revelation 21:27

    What is the *Lamb's book of life*?

4. The Books
    a. Daniel 7:9-10

    b. Revelation 20:12

    How are the dead judged?

Questions

5. Two choices, one decision. Eternity with Jesus or in the lake of fire with the devil.

   If you believe in Jesus, are you condemned to perish? Yes or No.

   Where is your name?

6. Go back and read John 3:16-17 at the beginning of this chapter.

   If you *do believe* this is all true, if you died in the next hour, what place will you be in for eternity? Why?

   If you *do not believe* this is all true, if you died in the next hour, what place will you be in for eternity? Why?

Chapter 19-2: New

Revelation 21:1-22:5

The God who made us can also remake us.

– Woodrow Kroll

READ

In your bible, read Revelation 21:1-22:5.

THINK

Read the above quote. Do you believe God uniquely created you, made you? If you do, explain your belief. If you do not, explain what you believe on how you were uniquely made.

How does this belief affect how you live, your life choices and how you view the world?

DO

Looking in Revelation 21:1-22:5 complete the following questions and activities.

Word Studies

Use a concordance to look up these words and write the definitions here.

1. New (Rev 21:1)

    What aspect of your life would you like to be brand new?

Cross – References

Look up the bible verse to learn more about the topic.

2. In Christ

    a. 2 Corinthians 5:17

        Describe someone who is in Christ.

Activities

For the following, think of something you had that was old and you replaced with something new.

3. A tangible item

    Old:

    Replaced with:

    Why I replaced it:

4. An attitude

    Old:

    Replaced with:

    Why I replaced it:

5. An opinion or point of view

Old:

Replaced with:

Why I replaced it:

6. A personality trait or characteristic

Old:

Replaced with:

Why I replaced it:

7. A spiritual belief

   Old:

   Replaced with:

   Why I replaced it:

8. Do you need to replace a spiritual belief? If yes,

   What is the belief you need to replace?

   What belief do you need to replace it with?

Chapter 20-2: Blessed

Revelation 22:6-21

A man may lose the good things of this life against his will; but if he loses the eternal blessings, he does so with his own consent.

– Augustine

READ

In your bible, read Revelation 22:6-21.

THINK

Read the above quote. What is your initial reaction to this quote? How do you give consent through indecision?

DO

Looking in Revelation 22:6-21, complete the following questions and activities.

Word Studies

Use a concordance to look up these words and write the definitions here.

1. Reward (Rev 22:12)

    How are rewards given out?

2. Dog (Rev 22:15)

    Dog – The word *dog* can be used as a literal meaning or figuratively. As a metaphor, it means a man of an impure mind.

    When you look at the word *dog* in the context of verse 15, which meaning do you think it is?

Exploring the words *name* and *mark*

3. Name: *used for everything the name covers.*
   (New Testament Greek Lexicon/biblestudytools.com)

    a. To see in context, read Revelation 22:4

4. Mark: *an imprinted mark; a scratch or etching.*
   (New Testament Greek Lexicon/biblestudytools.com)

    a. To see in context, read Revelation 13:16 and Revelation 14:9

5. You find a lost dog in your neighborhood. It is cold out and he is scared and shivering. Do you,

    a. Cover him with your jacket, talk to him softly and bring him to your home or a place where he will be safe?

    b. Mark him with your phone number and walk away.

Question - If you love someone and had to protect them, would you cover them with something, even maybe yourself? Or, would you mark them with an etching?

What does God do?

He covers you, in the name of Jesus.

He [Jesus] commanded us to preach to the people and to testify

that he is the one whom God appointed as

judge of the living and the dead.

All the prophets testify about him that everyone who believes in him

receives forgiveness of sins

through his name.

Acts 10:42-43

Chapter 21-2: The End Begins

When the author walks on the stage the play is over. God is going to invade all right – something so beautiful to some of us and so terrible to others that none of us will have any choice left. For this time it will be God without disguise. It will be too late then to choose your side.

– C.S. Lewis

Read the above quote. Did you choose your side? Which side and why did you choose it?

1. What is the book of Revelation about? Support your answer with what you have read in the bible.

You answered this before you began the first study and at the end of it. Look back at your answers and compare all of them.

2. What is the most memorable insight for you in the book of Revelation?

3. We are responsible for what we know. What will you do with the knowledge and insight you gained from studying the book of Revelation?

   What I know.

   What I will do with this responsibility.

Three Questions, Revisited

These are the three questions addressed at the beginning of this guide. You answered them after *The First Study*. Now, answer them again and support your answers with scripture. Then, go back and compare with your answers from after *The First Study*.

Question#1 – Is Revelation Literal or Symbolic Writing?

Question #2 – Is Revelation a Chronological Account?

Question #3 – Is Revelation Past, Present, or Future?

The Not-So-Impossible Book of Revelation, Revisited

Write your own last chapter to this guide. You can write a summary, list out your thoughts, draw your thoughts, or make a plan for your next steps in bible study. Write what is on your heart and mind about what you have learned. And remember,

> *Blessed is the one who reads aloud the words of this prophecy,*
> *and blessed are those who hear it and take to heart what is written in it,*
> *because the time is near.*
> Revelation 1:3

Books by Kathy Nosal

Bible Study
The Not-So-Impossible Book of Revelation

Aging
The Adult Child's Guide to Planning Your Aging Parents' Move

English as a Second Language (ESL)
The Little Guide for the New ESL Teacher

Just One Topic ESL Word Puzzles – Food Word Puzzles

Visit kathynosal.com for updates.

www.ingramcontent.com/pod-product-compliance
Lightning Source LLC
Chambersburg PA
CBHW081146040426
42445CB00015B/1783

* 9 7 8 0 5 7 8 4 3 6 8 3 8 *